From the Universe's Lips to My Ears

From the Universe's Lips to My Ears

First published by noopface in 2017

Second Edition

Contents

IV   Her

From the Universe's Lips to My Ears

From the Universe's Lips to My Ears

Written by noopface (Anup Sohanta)
Instagram: @noopface

All artwork by Broken Isn't Bad
Instagram: @broken_isnt_bad

A Special Thank You

To all of those people that have uplifted me, encouraged me and loved me without restriction. Thank you to my family, my friends, my supporters, to anyone who is seeking to raise their vibration and a special, thank you to "Her" I dedicate this to you. Thank you for the support, encouragement and love. I am eternally grateful.

Introduction

This book might not change your life (sorry) It is a collection of poetry and messages that I have written over the years, messages that the Universe has sent to me. I have allowed these messages to flow through me unrestricted at some point or other as various people or events have inspired me. I hope as a reader you relate to them, or find something within them that is deep within yourself; like a hand that dips into a stream pulling out gems, you wash away the dirt, leaving only the sparkling stones in your hand.

Around the start of 2011, I had just come out of a breakup and felt a little lost, I didn't know how to heal myself and all I did feel at the time was an enormous amount of pain, anger and confusion. I trusted the process that the Universe would eventually heal me, that "it just takes time" and all the usual things your friends tell you and that you eventually tell yourself. I asked the Universe for a sign; send me something, please, so I can stop feeling so awful, not just about the breakup but stuck and dissatisfied with my life in general. It responded. It didn't just respond with small trickles of rain from above, it hit me in the face at the speed of a space shuttle taking off at 18,000mph. I had a huge wake-up call, I started to allow new people into my life, new places and new experiences. I worked on myself and at the time I was reading books like The Tao of Wu by The Rza and The Power of Now by Eckhart Tolle. I was reading poetry by Rumi and Charles Bukowski. I felt like I had lost my way between the years of 2008 – 2010 and all of the events that had occurred in the past led up to me awakening myself again in 2011. The artistic side that I had hidden underneath had resurfaced and I wanted to explore the vast regions of my mind.

The years that followed that, I developed a lot more and the people and experiences in my life have helped me to do so. I started an Instagram around 2013 with writing on it, quotes of others and a few from myself, in the hope to help people and spread words like wildfire. I started to include more of my own writing on my account and during these periods of growth; I have been broken, thrown into the fire and come out forged stronger than before once more. A little more versed in the lessons that life viciously hurls at me I have been able to see light, like a cracked window with light that peers into a dark room. My growth hasn't always been bad, I have experienced love and joy and this too has enabled a lot of growth within myself. I have felt love for others, I have felt synchronicity and I have felt a greater connection to the Universe than ever before.

In the past year or two, I have met new people and written about them, I have explored the microcosm more and I have tried to delve deep into myself and the myriad of people and places have helped me examine who I really am and what I'm here for. I have been able to feel the life-force around me, that surrounds me like a blanket, in Chinese it is called Chi, in Sanskrit, they call it Prana, or in Star Wars, they just call it "The Force." There are a handful of people in particular that have helped me raise my vibration to a point where I'm now able to share these words in a book and not just on my Instagram account. Overwhelming love and support is the greatest thing I have felt over the last year and I hope that by reading my words you are able to shift any lower vibrations into higher energy patterns, your thoughts dictate your reality. We're all here to learn and to be tested. We're all here to bloom into our true gorgeous self.

I

Love & Compassion

"I'm going to travel the world with the love of my life. And when we're standing in awe at the breathtaking views, I'll thank the heavens for bringing me you."

– noopface

Love

I have loved and been loved, I have experienced pain and heartbreak. To experience love to its fullest you must also experience the downsides to it. There must be good times and bad times. I have felt the most overwhelming love from partners sharing themselves with me, learning new things about them and also in the process of discovering myself. I have felt love as a baby enters my family, with soft fingertips pressing onto my hand as it clenches, eager and ready to experience this world yet again. I have loved friends and even felt a sort of love for strangers. To think that out of the entire population of the planet that our fate is somehow converging with this person, we're sharing an interaction with them and to feel such love for them. It is a mind-blowing concept.

As humans, we need to think of love as more of a state of being as opposed to an emotion that one feels. If we can accomplish it as a state of being then all things become love, everything that you do becomes full of love and all things are love.

From the Universe's Lips to My Ears

Compassion

Compassion should be a huge fundamental of any person trying to attain a higher vibration. Actually, compassion should be an integral part of any individual just trying to be a decent human being. I always adore giving my time to people, especially if they are in dire need of it, to show them some compassion and to show them some love. Part of me always thought it was selfish because it became an exchange. I would do something for them but I wouldn't leave empty handed. The word "Mudit" in Sanskrit means a sympathetic joy and delight from helping people in need and gaining a sense of fulfilment from their happiness and well-being. Should you honestly give that homeless guy some change? what if he spends it on drugs or alcohol. That's usually your first thought, but what if he genuinely needs the money for food.

Should you help a friend or family member in their time of need? If you have the means to do so, you should. Perhaps that little bit of compassion will change someone's life and maybe it won't. At least it'll make you feel good and enrich your life.

"Love & Compassion"

Generosity

There's nothing sexier than a generous person, with their time, attention and affection. Willing to give all of their heart, speak all of their mind and bare all of their soul. Revealing to you their true self and always willing to share their gorgeous evolving self.

– noopface

Heartbeat

Every morning she climbs on top of me, lays her head on my chest and listens to my heartbeat. I'm blessed to have her and to be part of her experience on this big and beautiful world. It reminds me that today and every day that follows will be a good day.

- noopface

Big Appetite

I am hungry to experience it all. The world is big and my heart is even bigger.

– noopface

Merging

*Be with someone who makes adventures out of late night trips to the store. Be with someone who mindlessly reaches over to you just so they can feel the warmth of your skin on theirs. Be with someone who asks you if you slept well, if you've eaten and someone who can't fall asleep without hearing your sleepy "goodnight." Be with someone who brightens your Monday and motivates you to do better, to be better, someone that tells you that you're going to accomplish great things for the entire week. Be with someone that raises your vibration, helps you, teaches you, is humble enough to let you teach them and shares themselves with you. Be with someone that never makes you doubt that you're as gorgeous as the full moon on a clear night. There are many ways to say "I love you" and **you** deserve them all.*

– noopface

Affection

When I love, I love on the deepest level. I love you with all of my being. I shower you with affection because it's the only way I know how. I remember every single intricate detail about you from your childhood stories to your favourite drink. I remember everything you have shared with me. I want to make you laugh, make you things, buy you things, teach you things, I want you to teach me things, I want to kiss you all over from head to toe, make you orgasm and be supportive of all of your dreams. Come to me when you're feeling down or upset. Your anxiety is my anxiety, your problems are my problems and we fight through everything together. We are not separate, you and I, I am always with you.

- noopface

One Day

One day you'll meet someone funny and cool and kind, with an enormous heart; their words will make your heart beat faster and their touch will make your spine tingle just like your favourite songs do. You're gonna laze around in bed together and go on brunch dates and make pun jokes and they're gonna respond with another pun. You'll have nicknames and inside jokes. You'll share things with each other that you've never told anyone else. Your morning eggs with them will taste better than any meal you've ever had before and your coffee will taste even richer. They'll move the hair away from your face and kiss it all over on the days you're stressed and they will encourage you, all they will want for you is to accomplish spectacular things.

- noopface

Perfect Fit

Right now, there is someone out there wondering what it would be like to be with someone exactly like you. They're the perfect fit, they'd laugh at your bad jokes, they'd wanna get breakfast and lay around in bed all day. They would kiss you on the forehead on those days you're so overcome with anxiety and hold you until your worries feel like they've faded away. This is the one, the one you want to be with, the one you want to raise a family with and they would love you unconditionally, realigning all of the cogs in your soul on the days you feel broken.

Unfortunately, that person is most likely in a parallel universe. So good luck with that.

- noopface

I Am Here

You never have to hide from me. You can tell me anything and you don't have to pretend that everything is perfect when you're crumbling away inside. I am always here, always.

- noopface

The Soul Wants

The soul wants, what the soul wants. We can't force people to like us, love us or be with us. We put so much pressure on having a relationship with someone, that it becomes full of expectations and self-gratification. What can that person do for us and how good can they make us feel. To live in life's essence, it's more about sitting back and enjoying the ride, rather than forcing a connection. If the connection is meant to be, the Universe will pave the way.

- noopface

The Infinite Energy Loop

You deserve the lover that doesn't take from you, leaving you depleted. The lover that fires you up not puts you out. The lover that relays your energy back to you and it flows infinitely.

– noopface

Self Love

You are so amazing, so beautiful, an inspiration to others. Any one would be lucky to have you. I love you so much.
I repeat to myself in the mirror

- noopface

Stroke My Soul

Don't spend money on me to show me you love me. Spend your time, energy and effort. Show me compassion and treat me with respect and care. Above all else, massage my ego profusely.

- noopface

The Experience

Trust love enough to let someone in. Whether it works out or not. It was an experience.

– noopface

Interest

I like compassionate people. Kind people. A person that goes out of their way to speak to you. Someone that acts interested. Someone that is interested in everything you do and all that you are; the things that make you laugh, the places you want to visit, the music that makes you feel at home, the goals you've set for yourself in the future. Someone that conveys concern if you've given yourself ample nourishment during the day. Someone that will be there when you're raw and wild like thunder and lightning and you feel like everything is falling apart. I want that person.

- noopface

Sharing the Experience

It's all about that one person you think about when something touches your soul and you think 'they' would love that.

– noopface

My Home

And one day she'll say "on my way home" and when she walks through your front door you'll thank the heavens it never worked out with anyone else before that.

– noopface

My Open Heart

My heart is wild and chaotic. And at the same time it's serene, crystal blue waters under a dusty pink sunset. It's open and free to think and feel so much.

– noopface

The Unicorn

You don't control a unicorn, love her and let her be free. Treat her with the utmost care, tenderness and compassion. Only then will she share her magic with you.

- noopface

Spiritual Collaborator

Your partner has gotta be more than just a lover. They gotta be your best friend, your confidant, your spiritual collaborator and your teacher. They have to help you face the things you don't want to face alone. The person you eat with, laugh with and the person that makes you learn new things about yourself.

– noopface

Scars

I will pour myself into your scars so that no one can ever hurt you. I want to kiss every part of your body. Every part of your soul.

– noopface

Thank You

I'm sorry that I'm not always easy to love, I'm trying to improve myself. I want to thank you from the bottom of my heart, for always having the compassion to stay.

– noopface

Exquisite Sensation

I like weird people, broken people, the people with a little darkness inside of them and an enormous amount of light waiting to beam out of them. They are the fascinating ones, the ones I want to hear all about, the kinda person that goes out of their way for you and when they do decide to share themselves with you and open up to you it's the most exquisite sensation you'll feel. Show me the deep chasms in which you hide the real you and I'll show you there's nothing to fear.

– noopface

Cosmic Kiss

Kisses your bruises and scars, they're as beautiful as the stars.

– noopface

Love Thy Existence

I only want the lover with a heart as big as mine, an infinite container that never ceases to get full of love with life. With existence itself.

- noopface

Kindness

Is there anything more satisfying than doing something pleasant for someone you care about; almost like the good deed makes you feel intoxicated, and by doing good, you feel good, you'd do it ten times over just to see a big beautiful smile on their face. Please keep doing those things, pour your heart and soul out like molten rock and fill those enormous gaps in other people to make them strong again. You have a rare opportunity in this world to heal your lovers, friends and your family and in the process heal yourself. The greatest gift you will ever be able to give is kindness.

- noopface

Euphoric Love

Be with someone who doesn't get tired of hearing about your day, hearing about your interests and the things you're truly passionate about. Someone that vibrates with you, sets their intentions with you and wants to see you grow tall and free. Someone that you can be generous with your true self and unapologetic about who you are because that person will accept every single tiny miracle that you are composed of. Someone that you can do anything and everything with and feel euphoric love for being in the moment with 'that' person.

- noopface

Wish

Support those that you love, show them compassion, be the ladder to help them reach up and touch the sky and claim the stars as their own. For every star they bring back down is a wish.

– noopface

Evolution

Love me for everything that I am, for all of my mistakes and imperfections. For all of my insecurities and 'lack ofs' I am a human that needs work and is constantly evolving.

– noopface

Discovering a New Land

How could anyone ever treat you like that? How could they take you for granted, belittle you and make you feel unimportant? It's not a reflection of you, it's a reflection of how they feel about themselves. You're a thing of beauty and when I found you, it felt like I had discovered a new land that was full of magic, wonder, warmth and love. I feel like I've lived here my entire life and I'll never leave your side. I'm grateful you managed to get free because the Universe led you to me.

- noopface

Beautiful Glow

If you care deeply for someone you want all aspects to shine, every cell vibrating happiness and love in their body. You encourage their curiosity, their sense of adventure, play and the things they find really interesting. If they're excited about something you listen to them and pay attention, it's worth it just to see that big beautiful glow on their face.

– noopface

II

Pain

"Pain is part of the double-edged sword of life, sometimes we inflict it on ourselves or sometimes it's inflicted on us by others, either way, it's pretty shitty."

- noopface

Pain

Pain is an important aspect of life, you can let pain completely take over your life or you can use it as a plateau to reach a higher place. Pain and anger are two things that can rule your life if you don't keep them in check. You can let them consume you and wallow in self-pity, weeping on the floor, or you can let the pain teach a valuable lesson. You can learn from it and grow from it. The pain could come in many forms from your life's events; loss, betrayal, a sense of worthlessness, but you are important and your thoughts and feelings can be changed by you at any time. Be free from pain and sorrow like a child, who does not know it yet, that has never experienced it yet.

"Pain"

Demons

You turn off the lights and lay there in silence, the demons start crawling out from every crevice of your mind to torture you in the prison you have built for yourself.

– noopface

Molecules

Don't be sad about who has passed. Everyone has to die sometime, right? We're all molecules colliding against each other. We meet, we interact and we part ways and maybe, just maybe, we'll see each other again someday.

– noopface

The Phantom

At night I see your face
I smell your perfume
I taste your skin
I hear your laugh
I feel your hand holding mine

And then my heart sinks like
a brick in the ocean because
I'll never feel those things
again.

– noopface

Time

You think you'll never get over the unbearable pain of missing someone so much it feels like a part of you has gone. Eventually, you wake up and they're not your first thought in the morning and they're not your last feeling at night. You stop checking your phone hoping that the notification is from them and every time you think about them your heart won't skip a beat anymore either. You have everything inside of you to heal yourself. Their messages move further and further down your inbox as your soul begins the process of restoring yourself. You are important, wish them well on their journey because you have your own.

– noopface

Restoration of the Soul

I am an overthinker until it breaks me and in all of the pieces, I find myself. Again.

- noopface

III

The Universe, Adventure and Growth

"Hello world, I welcome the ecstatic experience. I am ready for new things. Big things."

– noopface

The Universe, Adventure and Growth

Keep on thinking those beautiful things, make your dreams even bigger, believe they will happen. Adventure and see more, take as much in as possible. If you want abundance, imagine it is already yours. The Universe is your guide, there is a Universe inside of you and it does everything in your best interests. The only thing is you can't swim against the current, you need to let the energy beam out of you. You can't manifest your dreams by thinking of negative thoughts all of the time. It is not an easy skill to hone, but you must become a state of being that feels in their soul that there is a larger force at play.

Growing is an important part of the human experience, as people, we need to grow and not just physically. All of the events that occur in our lives mould us into who we are. As people, we are constantly evolving and our souls are always evolving, new experiences with places and people give our character definition. The experiences in life are all lessons so that we can find ourselves again, who we truly are.

"The Universe, Adventure and Growth"

The Decorator

Decorate your consciousness with those big, beautiful dreams of yours and they will manifest.

– noopface

Routine

Every morning when you wake up, start your day with the thought "I'm going to do something wonderful today" it will become part of your morning routine and amazing things will always happen to you.

– noopface

The Gardener

There's no big secret to a happy life. You plant seeds of kindness everywhere and they grow. Of course, you must water them every now and again.

– noopface

The Living Flame

See the living flame within yourself and you will ignite it in others.

– noopface

The Cosmic Wind

Hang in there. One day the wind will carry you away and when you land on your feet, it will be the most glorious thing you've ever felt.

– noopface

Grateful

So here's to the lovers we thought we'd never get over, but we did. The scars we thought would never heal, but they did. The time we thought we'd wasted, but we learnt so much. The toxic thoughts of feeling like we're not enough but we learnt how to love ourselves. Thank you for making me who I am.

– noopface

Hand on My Shoulder

It's like one day everything is going okay and the next it's all falling apart faster than you can put it all back together. You get knocked down so many times, you become conditioned to take a hit, but you just keep going, keep pushing forward and eventually you learn to hit back. I'm glad someone was there, I'm glad that you were there to comfort me and tell me things were going to be okay, that everything would be alright and everything is granted from the Universe and if it goes, it wasn't meant for you anyway.

- noopface

Mistakes

Make mistakes, lots of mistakes. It's only after making mistakes and learning lessons that we're able to grow. Grow through pain like a plant grows through dirt and your being will come out blossoming.

– noopface

Trust

If you don't let go of the steering wheel every now and again you'll drive yourself insane.

- noopface

Reach

If things are always in your grasp, you are settling. You need to reach out from beyond your comfort zone. Don't settle for anything. Keep your head held high, your standards higher and your food so high no one else can get any.

– noopface

Snip Snip

Cutting people off is my favourite thing, to abruptly let someone know that they're not fit to be in your company. You find new people because you're emitting a different kind of vibe and people on the same wavelength start reaching out to you. It's pleasant, it's pleasant to not be trapped in a cycle of shitty people.

– noopface

Articulating Anger

Don't manage your anger, eliminate it by articulating it. This world is filled with people who allow anger to fester inside themselves, causing them more harm than good. Anger doesn't deserve to be managed, it should be eliminated from the body. Find a container or activity that helps you pour your heart, soul and frustration into and transform it into something positive.

– noopface

Support

I will totally support you while you're finding yourself. What I will not support is being taken advantage of to fuel your ego.

– noopface

The Chase

If I'm not good enough for you from the start, please don't chase me when I decide to move on because you were too foolish to see what was in front of you. That's just embarrassing.

- noopface

Embrace

When it comes embrace it, when it's time to let things go, let them go. Have faith in the Universe because it has faith in you.

- noopface

Seeing It All

Love until your heart is bursting at the seams. Adventure until your legs are aching and your soul is full to the brim. Your life will flash before your eyes; the past, present and future. Make sure that you didn't waste it.

– noopface

Wheel of Emotion

Love, pain, pleasure, happiness, sorrow. They're all connected. You have to feel all of them to truly live. You can't always feel happy and you won't always feel sorrow. Adventure and live your life, feel anything and everything.

- noopface

Gratitude

Convey gratitude for the lessons life viciously hurls at you. Be grateful for the bad times just as much as the good, the pain will enable growth and they will help you distinguish dark from light.

– noopface

Beautiful Garden

You are a garden filled with wild flowers and every garden takes time, effort, it takes love. Love and care for yourself and you will bloom for eternity, the sweet scent will linger out of your being and it will be absolutely intoxicating to others. Seeds that you have planted will grow into enormous trees and shade you from negativity and the roots will spread far and wide, giving you a greater connection to others and the Universe.

– noopface

Cosmic Cubs

One day when my children are sleeping I will kiss them on the face and tell them they were made from love, they will always be loved. They are little lions comprised of pure light and magic and I am always here to support them and build them up. Their happiness is like the elixir of life to me and they will accomplish miracles. They are my miracles.

- noopface

Energy Map

One day you'll wake up and it won't feel like you're walking through a dark tunnel anymore. You'll see all of the currents of energy that flow through you, all of the threads of current that make up the Universe and it will be the most beautiful thing you've ever seen. It'll all make sense, how everything is connected, like an enormous universal map.

- noopface

Conversing

The best conversations you'll ever have are with people you adore to bits about crazy shit like different dimensions, love, the destination of souls, conspiracies, the Universe, black magic and supernatural entities.

– noopface

My Adventure Journal

Adventure until you're writing a book with ink spilt throughout the pages of time, each chapter is a new day, new laughs, new people, time spent with existing connections and one day you'll see the back cover and feel so fulfilled and then write another book and another. You'll have an entire library filled with thoughts, feelings, places, people, love, heartbreak and laughs.

– noopface

Relax

If you're upset, relax. Everything will be okay. There's always another opportunity, another love, another person, another time. Revel in the small things, in the existence of living and taste the ripe fruit's of life that will bring a huge smile to your face and an even bigger smile to your heart. Eat nourishing foods, hear the laughter of a child, be kind to other people; do you see that inner glow you've given them? And how you've helped them on their journey. Love yourself, because you are the Universe, composed of tiny miracles and stars.

– noopface

Deserving

When you realise you deserve better, you are growing.
When you stop taking people's shit, you have grown.
When you channel negativity into positivity you are
thriving.

– noopface

Affirmation of the Day

Affirm to yourself that good things always come to you; always happen to you, good people always gravitate towards you and always be grateful for the things you have and the wonderful things that are yet to come.

- noopface

Shedding Skin

Out with the old, in with the new. That should be your stance on people. Shed toxic and disloyal people like skin; if they aren't giving you an emotional orgasm or a sexual orgasm, then they aren't a requirement for your life.

– noopface

New Beginnings

Thank you, Universe, for all of those people and places. Thank you for all of those experiences that pass through me, that create me. This is why I'm here, to find myself and create. I look forward to the many new people and adventures that are yet to come.

– noopface

Feels

Your thoughts and feelings are yours alone and they should pass through your stream of consciousness, they are only temporary and you can change them at any time. You can change how you feel about yourself and others. Be free and wild, like a young child that hasn't yet felt sadness and curious for the next adventure. The happier you are, the more happiness you will attract into your space and like-minded people will follow. You create your own world.

- noopface

The Light & Dark

The good days bring joy and the bad days bring experience but don't ever doubt that it's all important to your growth.

– noopface

Gems

Pay attention to those people that are there when you're down, that support your choices in the present and push for you to achieve your dreams. You don't have to face the journey alone, the people by your side are the real gems of this world.

- noopface

Checklist for Life

Things not to
do

- *Worry about what people think of you*
- *Let people's insecurities about themselves hold you back*
- *Give shitty people the benefit of the doubt*
- *Give your power away to people in an attempt to make them like you*
- *Let people crush your dreams because they think they're too big*
- *Douse yourself in something flammable every time something or someone pisses you off*

Things to
do

- *Always keep your head held high, always remember you are a creator*
- *Grow*
- *Grow*
- ***Keep growing, outgrow all of these bitches.***

  – noopface

Power

Whatever your goals are, however big your dreams may be...you will find the strength. Don't become attached to it, don't feel fear of losing it and you must certainly not feel any fear that you're not enough. All it takes is a simple thought that you can do it and act like you already have it. Ride the wave don't fight the current and you'll have everything you've ever wanted.

- noopface

The Grand Design

I see big things for you. Huge things. A destiny so bright it will make the world stop and stare in awe. Keep going and keep glowing.

– noopface

The Universal Chessboard

The Universe toys with us, like pieces on a chessboard. It consistently moves us to where we need to go and to who we need to meet. And if you trust it wholeheartedly without any resistance, the endgame will be everything you've ever dreamt of.

- noopface

Spiritual Nourishment

The link between nutrition and spirituality is a thing. Nourishing your body with high vibrational foods and plenty of water will have a positive effect on your soul. The more pollutants you disrupt your chi circuits with, the more blockages you will build up. You want the chi to run smoothly and openly and that will be beneficial to every aspect of your being.

– noopface

Keep Doing You

You shouldn't have to remind someone that you exist. If they want to be a part of your life they will make the time to do so.

- noopface

Bend the Knee

A beautiful mind and a passionate heart are the most luxurious things you'll ever own. You are royalty and it's time for the world to bend the knee.

– noopface

Soul Circuits

Do the things that light up the circuits in your soul and shine for the whole world to see.

– noopface

Breathing

Whenever you feel pain, anger or resentment; let the air around you completely fill your lungs, just breathe, let your inner-self breathe. This is your true self. There is a big world out there waiting for you, take all of the experiences you want, they're yours. You're still young, you're ineffably beautiful, incredibly smart and adventurous. Do more, be more, see more. There are many gifts out there waiting to enter your life so don't get tied down with those negative thoughts, they're only going to hold you back.

- noopface

The Universal Introduction

The Universe doesn't make mistakes, you don't just accidentally meet people. We are introduced to people we need. People to love us, for us to love them, people to cause us pain and piss us off, people that will be there waiting for you at the finish line when we're trying to overcome life's feats. There's something to be learnt from the exchange, whether it's a pleasant or an unpleasant experience for us, it is an experience nonetheless. The Universe 'creates' the serendipity, so whether you're feeling overjoy, love, anger, pain or loss, it all adds to you growing as a person and elevating the resonance of your soul.

– noopface

My Tribe

I am proud of those people that never gave up. Those friends, family members and lovers that always had the courage to keep going. You believe there is a bigger picture to life, you're pursuing your dreams, you're hanging in there to get everything you want, even when times get a little tough, you keep expanding and attaining. Your life might not change overnight, but no matter how small a feat is..everything starts with a thought. I am observing and I see you blossoming like a flower and flourishing like a garden.

- noopface

The Cosmos

As I lay back, floating in the sapphire blue sea of the Cosmos while it bathed me in all of its glory, it whispered into my being all of the beautiful things waiting for me.

- noopface

Fire

I was born of fire and back to fire I'll go.

– noopface

The Present Moment

The past fades and the future's not set in stone, so we must make the present moment our home.

– noopface

Deserving

May you never get bitter over the challenges life throws at you. You are meant for great things and what is meant for you will always be for you. Wear the feeling like a suit of armour and there isn't a single soul that can take that away from you. Own it and experience it. It is yours. This life and everything in it is for you. You deserve it.

- noopface

Hungry

I am hungry to experience it all. The world is big and my heart is even bigger.

- noopface

Allowing

Allow it fully with intention and what is meant for you will come. Don't chase and certainly don't beg, If it goes, wish it love on its way because it wasn't meant for you. Having total control over something or someone is suffocating for it and toxic for you. Just simply live in the present and live in the moment. Let the burning light inside of you be your guide and always look up to the vastness of the sky that's filled with golden opportunities. Never forget the stars, planets and moons also reside deep within you too.

- noopface

The Hive Consciousness

We're all broken people riddled with issues, holes, cracks, physical imbalances and emotional complexes. But there is a light inside of you that peers through the cracks and it is waiting to escape. Don't be afraid of it; mould it, shape it, it is yours and that is your true power. You're never alone in this world, the collective consciousness of the Universe streams through you. The hive consciousness, we are never apart and we are here to help.

- noopface

Equal Terms

Anyone that makes you jump through hoops for their affection just likes the attention from you and doesn't respect you in the slightest. You should always be on equal terms with each other. Never doubt your self-worth and they should never make you feel like you're not good enough. Politely tell them to go fuck themselves.

- noopface

Self Worth

Proving your worth is a tedious and toxic exercise. The right people will stay. They'll see all of the light radiating from you and they won't ask for anything other than to see you happy.

– noopface

Effort

If they're genuinely interested in being a part of your life, they'll make the effort and if they don't.. they're not worth the effort.

– noopface

IV

Her

*"I was always the moon and she was the open sea, a
timeless connection that was meant to be."*

– noopface

Her

There she was, the most unexpected serendipity that had happened to me in years. She had eyes like sapphire blue oceans, one could get lost if they dived down far enough. She radiated a gorgeous warmth about her, a very inviting warmth that pulled me in like gravity. She shared herself with me; her childhood, her life, her hopes and dreams and I was hungry for more. I realised I'd been starving my entire life, this beautiful soul, this ineffably beautiful woman made me feel full.

She had a thirst for knowledge and a lifelong quest for new adventures, seeking out new experiences and revelling in her existence, enjoying the variety and stimulation of seeing breathtaking places and meeting eccentric people. She was a wanderer, forever exploring and found solace on beaches and mountains where she could view the sea uninterrupted, the hidden depths of the sea would calm her fiery soul. Life signified new beginnings, new approaches and developing new abilities within herself. It empowered her to throw herself into the vastness of it all and look forward to everything yet to come.

She had the most profound impact on my life, sharing her spirituality with mine, sharing herself with me. It was the bonding of two souls and we began to merge, she was the mirror to me. A magical mirror to another plane of existence. She made me learn new things about myself every day. She had a huge influence on me and my being vibrated higher. Thank you for existing, you are a rare treasure that one could spend a lifetime trying to find.

"Her"

The Conqueror

She's the sort of woman you meet only when you're resonating at a certain frequency. If you can't match her high vibration then leave her the fuck alone, she's going to conquer the world.

– noopface

PDA

She loves a man who can grab her attention with his mind and grab her ass in public.

– noopface

I Will Find You Again

Of all the gifts in the ages; in all of the timelines, in all of the serendipities, you have been the most beautiful gift I could ever hope to receive. You are my home, my past, my present and my future. I am eternally grateful for your existence. You are my soul away from my soul, I will find you again and again.

– noopface

Strength

The demons you have faced became your motivation to vibrate higher, to attain a closer connection to the microcosm within yourself. You brushed off any doubts that people projected onto you and the challenges taught you great lessons along the way. You will conquer the entire world with your beautiful soul and vessel. Everything you were and all that you are radiates the power of 30,000 suns. I give you my love in all of its entirety, for you are the mirror that looks back at me. I'm so grateful that our timelines crossed again. And I'll be grateful every time they do.

I am so very proud of you.

– noopface

Transcendence

The world told her she couldn't. So she transcended anyway.

– noopface.

She Is the Universe

*She's not yours, or anyone else's, she never was. She belongs to the sky, the sea, the stars, the planets and the moon. She belongs to the Universe, **she is the Universe**.*

– noopface

The Creator

I want to kiss her legs and feet every morning, for every step she takes, she creates.

- noopface

The Big Bang

And even to this day, I remember our first encounter, you were like the mirror to me. I saw constellations in our eyes and planets in our mouths. A simple hello...and this is how the Universe was created.

– noopface

Queen

Strong willed. Soft heart. Alluring soul. A captivating mind. Always as sharp as a dagger. A true Queen.

- noopface

Third Eye

I kiss her forehead as she sleeps and direct my love to her third eye. I want her dreams to be as beautiful as she is.

- noopface

Morning Stretch

I love her most in the mornings with her messy hair, sleepy voice, stretching out like a lioness. And that look in her eye like she could eat me alive.

- noopface

My Kingdom

That feeling of being so comfortable with someone, your relationship with them is like finding that snug spot in bed. You just know that your souls have definitely met before, and not just in this lifetime, but you've encountered each other in many other lifetimes and a strange force always pulls the two of you back together. The familiarity of that smile, that laugh, those gestures, even the stupid arguments. It reminds you of a different time, a different era.

I guess what I'm trying to say is... She's my home, my kingdom, my Universe and I'd follow her into a thousand more lifetimes if it meant our souls could be together. If you have a place you call home, you should at least try to get there.

– noopface

Art

We talked about art; she talked about paints and planets, music and misery and I talked about her.

– noopface

Wasteland

You saw me as a barren wasteland with nothing to offer. She sees me as a newly discovered planet full of vast riches and infinite opportunities.

– noopface

Calamity

She thinks she's a calamity, that every single thing she touches turns to dust; always feeling like she tries so hard and it's never enough repeating a perpetual cycle of worthlessness, there's always another plot twist waiting around the corner to fuck her up.

She has forgotten who she is. That she's beautiful, that she's kind, that she's a Goddess and that everything that has ever come into contact with her has turned into gold, every person that has ever met her is blessed. Every path that she has ever deviated from is because the Universe is teaching her short term pain for long term gain. and it always, always has her best interests in mind.

- noopface

Thank You

Thank you for awakening those parts of me that had been dormant for so long. Thank you for plunging yourself head first into the depths of my being. Thank you for your love. Thank you for existing.

– noopface

Love Needs No Thanks

I love the intimacy when you share yourself with me. Your hopes, dreams, desires, what you're really passionate about. Tell me about your past, I want to laugh at your childhood photos. Tell me what the Universe spoke of when you were meditating and whatever else makes you happy. It will always be a pleasure for me to hear. I am here to support you, lift you up and encourage you and you never need to thank me because love needs no thanks. I will be forever grateful that you exist and the Universe guided you to me.

- noopface

Pasta

That individual right there. That's who I want to come home to. That's who I want to sit on the kitchen worktop and drink wine and taste my pasta sauce. There may even be making out, my hands cupping their gorgeous face while their cheeks go flush with excitement and love. (We're totally gonna make out.)

- noopface

Investment

The most lucrative investment I ever made was my time and love into you.

– noopface

Symphony

Tell me I'm amazing and the most beautiful soul you've ever encountered. Tell me everything I do is because the Universe will never lead me astray. Your voice calms me and the words only sound like a symphony coming from your mouth.

- noopface

Breakfast

Soft pecks on her lips gently as she gives me her morning doe-eyed look, my nose colliding against hers, my fingertips pressed into her silk like skin. My hand slides up the inside of her thigh as I lean in towards her ear, she yearns to hear my salacious words at the break of dawn, seductively I whisper "I made you breakfast."

- noopface

She Is Treasure

She is an adventure, with a soul full of fiery embers and a touch as calm as a passing breeze. She makes me feel like I've got it all figured out and also like there's still so much more treasure to discover. Be careful not to slip, or you may just fall for her forever.

– noopface

Gold

Every day she breaks off a little piece of herself and gives it to me, I treasure it with all of my being.

– noopface

Tender Touch

What a beautiful woman you are, with a tender touch and a fascinating mind.

– noopface

Dinner

Dinner, a lipstick stained wine glass and my soft lips on your neck as I slowly unzip your dress.

– noopface

That Laugh

You're attractive when you're laughing, but the passion in your eyes is an exquisite sight.

– noopface

Multiverse

You touched me past skin, past bone, all the way through into the essence of my being and it formed a new galaxy inside of me.

– noopface

Handful

I've liked you since I first laid eyes on you. You're beautiful, stubborn, gutsy and a bit of a handful.

– noopface

Scarlet Sunset

Sit near the edge of the cliff with me, let me feel the warmth of your hand on my cheek as a gentle breeze passes us by. Tell me all the things you'd never dream of telling anyone. The sunset is our only audience.

– noopface

The Meteors

Our souls impacted with one another's with enough force to wipe out an entire planet, you melted into me and I into you. Our fates would forever be intertwined.

– noopface

Those Evenings

Exchanging laughs and music and touches and fluids. There isn't anywhere on earth I'd rather be, than here. With you.

– noopface

Queendom

An inquisitive mind, a sharp tongue and a heart of gold. Nothing will stand in the way of her having everything she wants, for she roars like thunder and strikes like steel, she rules her Queendom and everyone kneels.

– noopface

Morning Cat

She always rolled around on the sheets; playful like a lion, ready to tear my clothes off in an instant and sink her claws into my skin.

– noopface

Anxiety

I'll be there when you're feeling low and need comfort after a bad day. When you have crippling anxiety, I will move the stray hair away from your eyes and squeeze you so tight. You'll come out of the fire forged stronger than before, I promise. Come to me.

– noopface

Hug Me from Behind

You ineffably beautiful woman, come to bed. Hug me from behind and whisper "you are mine."

– noopface

Your Soul

I think you are exceptionally beautiful, but I see past your physical appearance. You're a kind-hearted, gentle woman that makes me laugh and expresses herself to me.

– noopface

The Fire Inside Her

She had always kept the fiery embers of herself stored away. Most men weren't able to handle the naked flame and it would always result in them getting burnt. And then he came along. He cared for her in ways she had never felt before and encouraged the burning fire inside of her to grow and grow and it shouldn't ever be extinguished. For it was just as important as she is and should be nurtured. Just as she should be.

– noopface

Her Divinity

How can you be so perfect? so divine and so beautiful. Your heart is made of gold and moonlight and stardust. You rain down your love on me like a gift from the gods, that engulfs me like a blanket on a cold day. You are an ocean I want to get lost in, a mountain I want to be stuck at the top of, a planet I want to be stranded on. Consume me, devour me, I give myself to you completely.

– noopface

Blooming Babe

I watered her with my time, affection, love and attention. I've never seen a flower bloom so magically.

- noopface

"Her"

The Rare Rose

She took a sip of wine and uncrossed her legs revealing it all to me, a flower so rare that most men would spend an entire lifetime searching for it.

- noopface

A Taste

And once she gives you a taste of all the beauty and mystery she has to offer, you'll be starving for that woman for eternity.

– noopface

Hold Onto Her Tightly

And when she pushes you away to protect herself, hold onto her tightly and show her you're not going anywhere. Tell her there's no place on earth you'd rather be and anything she has to face she'll never face alone.

- noopface

Universe's Beautiful Creation

You are the Universe's most beautiful creation. From head to toe, you radiate the most exquisite glow.

– noopface

The Lioness

Above all else she is a mother. She is a lioness, loyal to her pride, full of strength and support. She nurtures those she loves with strong hands, capable hands that are able to do anything she commits herself to. Her touch is tender and gentle as if she were woven together with thread made of golden light.

– noopface

Wild & Free

She runs wild and free, I love all the parts of her my eyes can't see.

– noopface

Sharing Yourself

Tell me about your childhood, your future, sex, tell me about your experiences while being high, the music that sends a tingle down your spine. Share your library with me. I crave the unique complexities of your mind just as much as I desire your skin on mine.

- noopface

The Star

She is the star that navigates me home and my eternal anchor in the sea of consciousness. Fate kept bringing this beautiful woman back to me again and again, time after time, life after life.

– noopface

I See You

*Let's talk about everything. Be intimate with me. I want
you to fuck my mind. Let's talk about conspiracies,
spirituality, and the vastness of the universe. I want you to
tell me about the finer details of all of your aspirations; so
I can gently run my fingers through your dreams, the same
way I do with your hair. I don't just wanna talk about that
everyday shit.*

- noopface

The Hug

Having your soul around me feels like a tight hug and I never want you to let go.

– noopface

Multifaceted

Spiritual and kind with a filthy mind.

– noopface

Moonlit Whispers

Don't be surprised if the moon shines for you extra bright, I tell her about you every night.

– noopface

Wild

She kept me safe and I kept her wild, she had raw passion in her eyes and a playful smile.

– noopface

Orgasm of the Soul

*Whether we laughed, or played, or danced, or adventured together.
We were bound to one another past physicality, just being in the
presence of each other was an orgasm of the soul and all things
became sex and everything we did together was sex.*

- noopface

The Full Moon

My love, you are even more phenomenal than the full moon dripping down its pure light on all of those hopeful faces looking up to you.

- noopface

Perfect Being

I never saw any flaws, all I ever saw when I looked at her was a radiant being and there wasn't a word in any language to describe how perfect she was.

- noopface

Astral Plane

She grabbed me by the hand as I looked upon her face, she took me to a plane outside of time and space.

– noopface

The Encounter

Nothing happens by accident. Everything is written in the sky, the stars, the planets and the entire cosmos. Who knew that two strangers encountering one another could be such a gift.

– noopface

Incarnation

She is the incarnation of love itself. My home, my kingdom, my past, my future and my gift. Every lifetime, every age, I will find you. I will get to you and that's a promise I'll never break.

– noopface

Free

I'm lying down on the grass, content with my life, I have no worries and I have everything I have ever dreamed of. I'm sipping champagne, the sky is a gorgeous shade of blue and it's a gift to be here, with you.

– noopface

Majestic Mirror

You have such a big influence on me. You're a gateway, a mirror and I look at you and see a nebula full of beautiful things, things in you... things in me. I'm going to treasure waking up to your soul every morning.

– noopface

Disco Diva

She has an aura that can captivate an entire room, an alluring presence that conveys the power within her. She roams wild and free experiencing new things and meeting new souls leaving them better than how she found them. She treats life as a gift and she's head over heels in love with it.

– noopface

Complex Creature

Perhaps you have a multitude of layers and you are far more complex than most can grasp. Your beauty extends deeper than your skin. You are a labyrinth and I want to get lost on every single level.

- noopface

Deep Blue

*I looked at her and saw everything I found unique and mysterious
and magnificent in the world; the deep blue oceans in her eyes,
cheeks shimmering like the most beautiful of sunsets, lips as if
there were roses emerging from her mouth. She had hair like the
mane of a lion, glowing from her head like the stars glow on a
clear night. This woman was truly extraordinary, all she yearned
for was to wander and be free.*

- noopface

Divine Pairing

We are a divine pairing and we share a symbiotic rela-
tionship of two souls bound to one another. She is air and
I am fire. The perfect compliment to one another. She
gives me life and makes me grow, fuelling my passion
and making me so big that I feel unstoppable. In return I
give her my warmth, she gently rises and grows, reaching
higher places than she has ever reached before. Until she
can see the entire world.

- noopface

Pleiades

I could lie here for hours just counting the freckles on your face and kissing it all over. Tracing lines and geometric patterns over your body with my fingertips. There are no flaws on your body for every blemish and stretch mark is a thing of beauty to me. I must have finally accumulated enough good karma to have you here and you're all mine. A present from the Universe.

- noopface

Unification

Her smile brings me to my knees, not at her mercy but because I worship the ground she walks on. She deserves a love full of fire and zest and passion. Someone that loses sleep over her. Someone that has a love so deep for her he aches for her touch, for her conversation and for her mind to melt into his in unification.

– noopface

A Thousand Kisses

I planted a thousand kisses all over your face like seeds, so you'll grow to love yourself the way that I love you.

- noopface

The Promise

I promised I would meet you in the next life and the next and the one after that too. And if I were ever late, to speak to the Moon and she would lead me to you.

- noopface

Well, that brings me to a close for this snippet of my life. Thank you for taking the time to read my words and allowing me to share myself with you. I hope that by reading my book you have taken something insightful away that you can relate to.

Made in the USA
Monee, IL
08 January 2021